MULES
IN AMERICAN HISTORY

Norman D. Graubart

PowerKiDS press

New York

Published in 2015 by The Rosen Publishing Group, Inc.
29 East 21st Street, New York, NY 10010

First Edition

Editor: Amelie von Zumbusch
Photo Research: Katie Stryker
Book Design: Colleen Bialecki

Photo Credits: Cover © North Wind Picture Archives; p. 4 Universal Images Group/Getty Images; p. 5 Lorcel/Shutterstock.com; p. 7 Incomel/iStock/Thinkstock; p. 8 Pablo Blazquez Dominguez/Getty Images; pp. 9, 14 Culture Club/Hulton Archive/Getty Images; p. 10 Roger Viollet Collection/Getty Images; p. 11 SuperStock/Getty Images; p. 12 Fotosearch/Archive Photos/Getty Images; p. 12 (bottom) Lambert/Archive Photos/Getty Images; p. 12 (top) Nancy Brammer/iStock/Thinkstock; p. 18 Margaret Bourke-White/The LIFE Picture Collection/Getty Images; p. 19 Hunter Martin/Getty Images Sport/Getty Images; p. 21 John Moore/Getty Images; p. 22 Rigucci/Shutterstock.com.

Library of Congress Cataloging-in-Publication Data

Graubart, Norman D.
  Mules in American history / by Norman D. Graubart. — First edition.
      pages cm. — (How animals shaped history)
  Includes index.
  ISBN 978-1-4777-6769-6 (library binding) — ISBN 978-1-4777-6770-2 (pbk.) — ISBN 978-1-4777-6629-3 (6-pack)
  1. Mules—United States—Juvenile literature. 2. Mules—History—Juvenile literature. I. Title.
  SF362.G73 2015
  636.1'83—dc23
                        2013049618

Manufactured in the United States of America

CPSIA Compliance Information: Batch #WS14PK5: For Further Information contact Rosen Publishing, New York, New York at 1-800-237-9932

CONTENTS

CARRYING LOADS

When you picture a horse, you might imagine it galloping through an open field. After all, horses are known for their speed. What would you picture a mule doing, though? You might think of it carrying something on its back. Unlike horses, mules are not known for their speed. They are famous for their ability to carry and pull objects. Animals that do this are called **draft animals**.

This image shows a pair of mules pulling a wagon through the Cumberland Gap. In the early nineteenth century, settlers passed through the gap on their way to Kentucky.

Mules are less skittish, or easily spooked, than horses are. They are also thought of as more stubborn. However, this is mostly because they are smart and cautious.

Americans have been using mules for thousands of years. Farmers used them to pull plows and carry crops to the market. Their sure-footedness made mules perfect for working in **mines** or carrying loads over rough ground.

Mules look a lot like horses. They also look like donkeys. This is because every mule has a horse mother and a donkey father. The only way to make a mule is for a female horse and a male donkey to **mate**.

Mules are often about as big as horses. They can weigh up to 1,600 pounds (726 kg). They also have tall, pointy ears, which look like donkey ears. Mules can carry weight for a very long time without getting tired. This ability is called **endurance**. Mules have better endurance than horses. Mules can carry more than donkeys since they are bigger.

Male mules are often known as john mules, while females are called molly mules.

MULES FROM SPAIN

The first mules in North America were bred from horses and donkeys that Christopher Columbus brought with him from Europe. Over the next century, Spanish explorers, farmers, and merchants brought mules into New Spain. This Spanish **colony** included Mexico, Central America, and the American Southwest.

Spain was and still is known for breeding excellent mules. This mule carrying a load of cork bark is near Alcalá de los Gazules, Spain.

Over time, the Native Americans in areas settled by the Spanish began to use mules, donkeys, and horses, too.

The Spanish used mules to do many kinds of tasks. Mules pulled farm **equipment** and carried goods to the market. They even brought silver and gold from Spanish mines to big cities. Spanish settlers also used mules for riding, in addition to horses. Riding mules were usually females, while the work animals were usually male.

Did you know that George Washington helped make mules popular in the United States? In the 1780s, American donkeys were too small to make strong mules. Washington asked for help. The king of Spain sent him a large Spanish donkey, named Royal Gift. He used it to breed powerful mules.

Washington is called the father of his country because he was the first president and led the Continental army during the American Revolution. He is also considered the father of the American mule!

By 1808, the United States was home to around 855,000 mules. Some worked on farms. Others helped pull boats on man-made waterways called **canals**. The mules walked on towpaths that ran alongside the canals. Americans built several canals in the early nineteenth century. Canals made it easier to move goods and **raw materials**.

1495

Christopher Columbus brings several donkeys and horses, which will be used to breed mules, to the New World.

1785

King Carlos of Spain sends George Washington several donkeys to use in breeding mules.

1450   1500   1550   1600   1650   1700

1848

Gold is discovered in California. Mules will become important in the gold rush that follows.

1864

The Union army buys more than 87,000 mules to be used in military campaigns against the Confederacy.

1967

The American Donkey and Mule Society is founded to celebrate mules and donkeys in American culture and history.

1750   1800   1850   1900   1950   2000

1936

A mule called Mr. Jackson becomes the first official mule **mascot** for the United States Military Academy's sports teams.

1954

For the first time, there are more tractors than horses and mules on American farms.

As Americans moved west in the nineteenth century, they brought mules with them. Missouri was considered the opening to the west. Many American settlers went through Missouri to move west. It became a place where they picked up mules for the trip. Missouri mules were usually as big as horses but had the endurance of donkeys.

This illustration shows a mule train pulling a wagon across the Great Plains during the mid-nineteenth century.

MAP OF TRAILS FOR WESTWARD EXPANSION

British North America

United States

Oregon City

Sacramento

Salt Lake City

Council Bluffs

Nauvoo

Independence

Los Angeles

Santa Fe

Mexico

Key
— Mormon Trail
— Oregon Trail
— California Trail
— Old Spanish Trail
— Santa Fe Trail

This map shows the main trails settlers followed on their journeys west.

For wagons that carried very heavy loads, the settlers used mule trains. These were teams of mules that were all connected by ropes to the same wagon. Once the settlers got to their new land, the same mules were used for farm and ranch work.

15

Mules had many kinds of jobs out west. They had the strength and patience to walk carefully in the rocky, hilly parts of states like Colorado, Montana, and Utah. This was helpful for farmers who lived in hard-to-reach places. It was also useful to companies that mined for silver, gold, and other minerals.

American settlers discovered gold in California in 1848. This led to the gold rush. Thousands of Americans moved to California, hoping to find gold. Mules were used in the gold mines. They also carried mail back and forth from the **boomtowns** that were built all over California.

This photo of a gold miner and his helpful mules was taken in Nevada during the mid-nineteenth century.

Before modern **technology**, the military used animals in war. Mules were used to carry guns, supplies, and soldiers. They were especially important during the Civil War. For example, they hauled floating bridges called **pontoon bridges**. When a big group of soldiers reached a river that they needed to cross, the

This photo of a US Army signal corpsman leading a mule was taken during World War II. The mule is carrying radio equipment.

You can see the United States Military Academy's mule mascots at sporting events in which cadets from the academy take part.

soldiers would place boats in the river. Then they placed wooden beams across the boats, forming a pontoon bridge.

Mules served in both World War I and World War II. Because of their important role in American military history, mules are the official mascot of the United States Military Academy.

The military no longer needed thousands of mules to carry supplies once trucks were invented. Farmers and ranchers also bought and raised fewer mules as farm technology improved. Instead of draft animals like mules or oxen, motorized tractors became the symbol of American farming.

Mules are still bred for pleasure riding. You can see mules at work in the rugged mountains of the American West. Riding a mule is one of the best ways to explore the area's canyons and mountains. In California, several groups use mules to carry hiking gear while hikers climb up the mountains of the Sierra Nevada.

Here, a national parks worker leads a string of mules along a path through the Grand Canyon, in Arizona. The mules are carrying supplies to be used to repair trails.

While mules are not used as often today, they are still important animals. There is even a town in Arizona called Supai that uses mules to deliver mail! Cars cannot drive into the town because it is in the Grand Canyon.

Mules are in no danger of dying out as a species. Remember, horses and donkeys need to mate to make a mule. There are plenty of horses and donkeys all over the world!

Mules are thought to be the world's most common hybrids. Hybrids are animals whose parents are two different species, or kinds, of animals.

boomtowns (BOOM-townz) Towns that got rich or grew very quickly.

canals (ka-NALZ) Man-made waterways.

colony (KAH-luh-nee) A new place where people move that is still ruled by the leaders of the country from which they came.

draft animals (DRAFT A-nuh-mulz) Animals that are used to move heavy loads.

endurance (en-DUR-ints) Strength and the ability to go long distances without getting tired easily.

equipment (uh-KWIP-mint) All the supplies needed to do an activity.

mascot (MAS-kot) A person, an animal, or an object that stands for a group of people.

mate (MAYT) To come together to make babies.

mines (MYNZ) Pits or underground tunnels from which stones or metals are taken.

pontoon bridges (pahn-TOON BRIDJ-ez) Bridges that float on water.

raw materials (RAW muh-TEER-ee-ulz) Basic things from which other things can be made.

technology (tek-NAH-luh-jee) Advanced tools that help people do and make things.

WEBSITES

Due to the changing nature of Internet links, PowerKids Press
has developed an online list of websites related to the subject
of this book. This site is updated regularly. Please use this link
to access the list:
www.powerkidslinks.com/anhi/mule/